My Sikh Year

Cath Senker

HODDER
Wayland

an imprint of Hodder Children's Books

Titles in this series

My Buddhist Year • My Christian Year • My Hindu Year
My Jewish Year • My Muslim Year • My Sikh Year

Conceived and produced for Hodder Wayland by

Nutshell
MEDIA

Intergen House, 65–67 Western Road, Hove, BN3 2JQ, UK
www.nutshellmedialtd.co.uk

Consultant: Rajinder Singh Panesar
Editor: Alison Cooper
Inside designer and illustrator: Peta Morey
Cover designer: Tim Mayer

Published in Great Britain in 2003 by Hodder Wayland, an imprint of Hodder Children's Books.

British Library Cataloguing in Publication Data
Senker, Cath
My Sikh year. – (A year of religious festivals)
1. Fasts and feasts – Sikhism – Juvenile literature
I. Title
294.6'36

ISBN 0 7502 4054 7

Printed in Hong Kong by Wing King Tong.

Hodder Children's Books
A division of Hodder Headline Limited
338 Euston Road, London NW1 3BH

Acknowledgements: The author would like to thank Amar Singh, Nina Manpreet Kaur Singh and Gurpreet Singh; Mohan Singh Nayyar, General Secretary of Gurdwara Sri Guru Singh Sabha, and Gurmukh Singh from the Sikh Missionary Society for all their help in the preparation of this book.

Picture Acknowledgements:
Art Directors & Trip Photo Library 14, 22 (H. Rogers); Chapel Studios 16 (Zul Mukhida); Circa Photo Library *Title page* (John Smith), 4 (B.J. Mistry), 9 (John Smith), 23 (Twin Studio), 26, 27 (John Smith); Prodeepta Das 8, 17; Paul Doyle *Cover*, 10, 15; Eye Ubiquitous 11 (Tim Page), 21 (David Cumming); Hodder Wayland Picture Library 20; Impact Photos 6 (Mohamed Ansar), 19 (David Harding); Nutshell Media 5 (Yiorgos Nikiteas); World Religions 7, 12 (Christine Osborne), 13 (Prem Kapoor), 18 (Gapper), 24, 25 (Christine Osborne).

Cover photograph: Carrying the Sikh flag in a procession for Vaisakhi.
Title page: A procession to celebrate Guru Nanak's Birthday.

Contents

A Sikh life

Sikhs believe in one God. They follow the teachings of their Gurus. A Guru is a holy teacher. The Sikh holy book is the Guru Granth Sahib. It is read out at festivals.

Sikhs believe all people are equal. They think that all religions should be respected, and that everyone should help other people.

These are the ten Sikh Gurus. They all helped to develop the Sikh religion.

This is Amar. He has written a diary about the Sikh festivals.

Amar's diary
Wednesday 3 April

My name's Amar Singh. I'm 8 years old. I live with my dad, mum, grandmother and sister. My sister's called Kiran Kaur and she's 5. My family's from India. I love playing football and cricket. At school I like games the best. At home, I like playing on the computer, drawing and playing with my cars. Because I'm a Sikh, I don't cut my hair.

To show respect to God and to their religion, Sikhs do not cut their hair. Many Sikh men wear a turban.

This Sikh symbol is called the Khanda.

At the gurdwara

Sikhs meet at the gurdwara to pray and learn about their religion. When they arrive, they take off their shoes and cover their heads.

People pray in the worship hall. They sing hymns (this is called kirtan), and listen to a reading. Everyone has karah parshad – a special sweet. Then they enjoy a tasty shared meal, called langar.

In this gurdwara, you can see the Guru Granth Sahib covered by a cloth on the left. A woman is bowing to it to show respect.

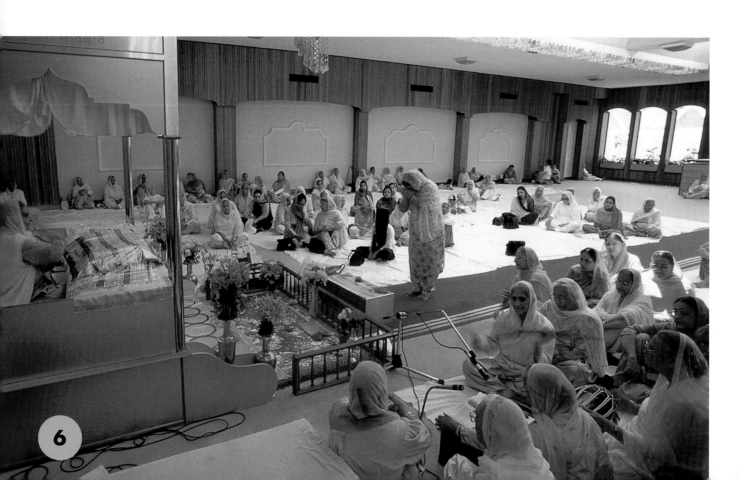

Sikhs take it in turns to cook and serve langar after worship.

Amar's diary
Sunday 7 April

Today I went to the gurdwara with Dad, Mum, Kiran and Grandma. When we went in, we bowed down to pay our respects to the Guru Granth Sahib. We all prayed together in the big hall. Then we ate langar. We had yoghurt, rice, sweet rice, roti (bread), dhal (spiced lentils) and salad. My favourite food at the gurdwara is the dessert, the kheer.

For Sikhs, every day is a special day, so there is no particular day for worship. In Western countries Sikhs usually go to the gurdwara on Sundays.

Sikh festivals

There are two kinds of Sikh festival: melas and gurpurbs. A mela is like a fair. It is a time for prayer and also a chance to have some fun!

The most important mela is Vaisakhi. The others are Divali and Hola Mohalla.

These bhangra dancers are celebrating Vaisakhi.

This procession in India is to celebrate Guru Nanak's Birthday.

Gurpurbs are festivals to honour Sikh Gurus. Sikhs celebrate on the anniversary of the Gurus' births and deaths. The most popular gurpurbs are Guru Nanak's Birthday and Guru Gobind Singh's Birthday.

Amar's diary
Thursday 11 April

My favourite festival is Vaisakhi because we get lots of presents and sweets! We always do bhangra dancing at Vaisakhi. It's great fun. Sikhs have festivals to celebrate the birthdays of the Gurus. My favourite is Guru Gobind Singh's Birthday, when I play my drum at the gurdwara. The Gurus are important to us because they teach us the right way to live.

Vaisakhi: New Year

April

Vaisakhi is the most important mela. It marks the Sikh New Year. At Vaisakhi, Sikhs remember how their community, the Khalsa, first began.

On the festival day, people start by bathing. They pray quietly at home. Then they go to the gurdwara. They listen to a service about the Khalsa.

A procession in England to mark the Sikh New Year. You can see the Sikh symbol, the Khanda, on the flag.

SYMBOL OF SIKHISM

This boy is joining the Sikh community in a special ceremony. He sips Amrit five times. It is also sprinkled on his eyes and hair.

At Vaisakhi, Sikhs welcome new members to their community. Holy sugar water called Amrit is sprinkled on them. They promise to follow the Gurus' teachings.

Amar's diary

Saturday 13 April

Today it was Vaisakhi. We celebrated at home and in the gurdwara. At home we prayed together and Grandma made lots of sweets for us. Then we gave each other presents. I got a new toy and some new pyjamas, and so did Kiran. We played with our new toys for a bit and then we went to the gurdwara. At the gurdwara we had some fruit and said our prayers.

Vaisakhi celebrations

Outside every gurdwara hangs the Sikh flag, the Nishan Sahib. At Vaisakhi, Sikhs take down the flag-pole and flag. They wash the pole in yoghurt to make it pure. They cover it with a fresh, new cloth and put on a new flag.

Everyone cheers as the clean flag-pole is raised! The Nishan Sahib flies high again.

Groups of people perform bhangra dancing outside the gurdwara. There may be sports, arts and music competitions.

The flag-pole, with its new cloth and flag, is raised outside the gurdwara.

A display of Sikh martial arts at Vaisakhi. Martial arts are very important to Sikhs.

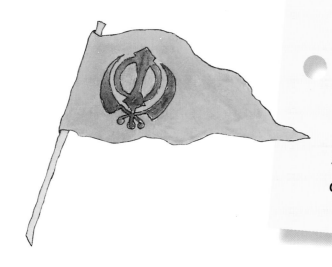

Amar's diary
Sunday 14 April

Yesterday at Vaisakhi we watched the new flag-pole being raised outside the gurdwara. Then competitions were held. I drew a picture of people going on a sponsored walk, but I didn't win anything. Dad and I joined the bhangra dancing. I wore my kurtah pyjama, our traditional costume, but Dad wore jeans. Dad put Kiran on his shoulders while he was dancing and Mum joined in, too.

Martyrdom of Guru Arjan

May/June

At this gurpurb, Sikhs remember Guru Arjan, their fifth Guru. He became a martyr for spreading the Sikh religion.

Guru Arjan was tortured. He was soaked in boiling water and had baking hot sand poured over him. He was not allowed to drink any water. Yet he died calmly.

A picture of Guru Arjan. He put together the first Sikh holy book, the Adi Granth.

Sikhs in England give out free drinks to remember Guru Arjan.

In Guru Arjan's memory, Sikhs give away cool drinks to everyone. In India it is hot at the time of this gurpurb so the cool drinks are very welcome.

Amar's diary
Saturday 26 May

Today was the festival to remember Guru Arjan. At the gurdwara, people gave out kachi lassi – it's half milk and half water, with some sugar added. Some years there is fruit juice instead. At my school there are Sikhs, Christians, Jews, Hindus and Muslims. We talked about how everyone should be able to follow their own religion in peace.

The Guru Granth Sahib

August/September

Sikhs hold this festival to celebrate their holy book.

In 1708 Guru Gobind Singh, the tenth Guru, decided there would be no more human Gurus. The holy book, the Adi Granth, was to be the only guide for Sikhs. Its new name was the Guru Granth Sahib.

Men and women may read from the Guru Granth Sahib in the gurdwara.

Amar's diary

Monday 19 August

Today was the festival for celebrating our holy book, the Guru Granth Sahib. It's written in our Punjabi language. When it's written down it's called Gurmukhi. I can't read it myself, but Grandma and Dad can. In the gurdwara, we look after the Guru Granth Sahib. We bow to it and pray to it. When we're not using the book, we cover it and put it in a special place.

A special fan called a chauri is waved over the Guru Granth Sahib to show respect.

At this festival, Sikhs worship in the gurdwara. They think about how they can follow the teachings of their holy book more closely.

Divali

October/November

Divali is a festival of light. Sikhs celebrate the time when their sixth Guru, Har Gobind, was freed from prison. When he arrived at the holy city of Amritsar, Sikhs lit candles and oil lamps to welcome him.

Since then, Sikhs have always celebrated with lights and fireworks. They light fairy lights, or clay lamps called divas.

These Sikhs in England are burning candles outside their gurdwara to celebrate Divali.

Amar's diary

Friday 19 October

Yesterday was the end of Divali. Mum and Dad gave me a Manchester United shirt and Grandma gave Kiran and me lots of sweets. We knew it was a special day because we normally only get one sweet a day. We went to the gurdwara and I lit a candle. Outside the gurdwara there was a brilliant firework display. I watched it with my friends.

This man is handing out Indian sweets at Divali.

People dress in new clothes and give each other boxes of Indian sweets. There is music and dancing. In the evening, prayers are held at the gurdwara.

Guru Nanak's Birthday

November

This is a very important gurpurb. Guru Nanak was born in 1469. He started the Sikh religion.

In Britain there are fairs with stalls and games to celebrate this day. In India there are lively processions.

Guru Nanak (second from the right) with two followers and two of his sons.

The Akhand Path reading finishes on the morning of the festival.

Amar's diary
Sunday 19 November

Yesterday was Guru Nanak's Birthday so we went to the gurdwara to pray. I listened to the end of the Akhand Path reading. Grandma was at the gurdwara for most of the day. I came home after two hours. We were told how Guru Nanak started our religion and what he taught the Sikhs. There was lots of food – and sweets, too. We could eat and drink as much as we wanted!

In the gurdwara, just before the festival begins, Sikhs take it in turns to read aloud from the Guru Granth Sahib. Reading the holy book all the way through is called Akhand Path. It takes about two days and two nights!

Martyrdom of Guru Tegh Bahadur

December

At this gurpurb, Sikhs remember the martyrdom of Guru Tegh Bahadur, their ninth Guru.

Over 300 years ago, the emperor of India tried to force all Indians to become Muslims. Guru Tegh Bahadur gave his own life to help to stop this.

Guru Tegh Bahadur believed people should be free to choose the religion they wanted to follow.

Young Sikhs take part in a procession for this gurpurb.

This festival is mainly celebrated in New Delhi, in India. There are big processions. Sikhs walk to the large gurdwara that was built where the Guru was killed.

Amar's diary

Thursday 20 December

Yesterday we remembered the martyrdom of Guru Tegh Bahadur. At the gurdwara, we found out that he gave his life to help other people. The granthi who led the service told us how brave the Guru was. We talked about being kind to other people and helping them. I always try to help my friends if they find something difficult in football that I can do easily.

Guru Gobind Singh's Birthday

December/January

This gurpurb is in memory of Guru Gobind Singh, the tenth Guru. He taught that there was only one God. He said that Sikhs should pray every day and help needy people.

These young Sikhs are learning to play the harmonium (front of picture) and the tabla.

Guru Gobind Singh was very good at writing music and poetry. At the gurdwara, Sikhs sing and play some of his hymns.

There may be games and sports competitions. People send each other greetings cards to mark the Guru's birthday.

The five Sikhs leading this procession stand for the first five members of the Sikh community.

Amar's diary
Saturday 5 January

Today we celebrated Guru Gobind Singh's Birthday. Guru Gobind Singh told us always to wear the five Ks. These are: Kangha (comb), Kara (steel bangle), Kesh (uncut hair), Kachera (shorts) and Kirpan (sword). I'm still too young to carry a Kirpan. We performed some of the Guru's songs at the gurdwara. I played my dhol - a kind of drum. Dad taught me how to play.

Hola Mohalla

March

This festival celebrates springtime. In the past, the festival was a time when Sikhs trained for battle. Today, Sikhs still feel it is important for men and women to be strong and fit. They hold sports competitions and play games.

A display of martial arts at Hola Mohalla.

A man performs a show at Hola Mohalla in Anandpur, in India.

In the gurdwara, Sikhs read through the Guru Granth Sahib. They pray to keep healthy and strong.

Amar's diary
Sunday 31 March

My cousin Surinder has just come back from Hola Mohalla in India. She said there were mock battles, but no one really got hurt. Some people did clever tricks, like riding on a horse standing up! Then there were music and poetry competitions. They prayed, too, and on the last day there was a procession. Surinder said the langars at the festival were delicious.

Sikh calendar

April (3 days)
Vaisakhi
Sikhs remember how their community first began.

May/June (3 days)
The martyrdom of Guru Arjan
Sikhs remember their fifth Guru, Guru Arjan.

August/September (3 days)
The Guru Granth Sahib
The celebration of the Sikh holy book.

October/November (1 or 3 days)
Divali
The festival of light. Sikhs celebrate the time when their sixth Guru, Har Gobind, was freed from prison.

November (3 days)
Guru Nanak's birthday
At this festival Sikhs remember Guru Nanak, who started the Sikh religion.

December (3 days)
The martyrdom of Guru Tegh Bahadur
Sikhs remember how their ninth Guru, Guru Tegh Bahadur, gave his life to defend others.

December/January (3 days)
Guru Gobind Singh's birthday
People sing and play hymns that were written by Guru Gobind Singh, the tenth Guru.

March (3 days at Anandapur; 1 day everywhere else)
Hola Mohalla
The Sikh spring festival, with sports and games.

Glossary

Adi Granth The first Sikh holy book.

Akhand Path The non-stop reading of the Guru Granth Sahib from beginning to end.

Amrit Holy water that is given during the Sikh baptism ceremony.

bhangra A dance from the Punjab in India.

dhol A drum with two sides, played with the fingers. It is often played in bhangra music and at weddings.

divas Lamps that use wicks made from twisted cotton dipped in melted butter. Many divas are lit at Divali.

granthi The person who takes care of the Guru Granth Sahib.

gurdwara The building where Sikhs go to meet and worship.

gurpurb A festival to remember the birth or death of a Guru.

Guru A holy teacher.

Guru Granth Sahib The Sikh holy book. It is seen as a living Guru.

honour To show admiration and respect for a person.

karah parshad A sweet made from semolina, butter and sugar. It is blessed and then everyone is given some.

Khalsa The Sikh community.

kheer An Indian dessert made from rice, milk and sugar.

kirtan Singing hymns from the Guru Granth Sahib.

kurtah pyjama A long cotton shirt and cotton trousers. This is a traditional Sikh costume.

langar The dining hall in the gurdwara, and the free food people eat there.

martial arts Sports that use fighting skills, such as judo and karate.

martyr A person who is killed because of their religion.

martyrdom The death of a person because of their religion.

mela A word that means 'fair'. It is used to describe festivals that are not gurpurbs.

Nishan Sahib The Sikh flag that flies outside the gurdwara.

reading A part of the Guru Granth Sahib or another Sikh religious book. It is read out to people in the gurdwara.

tabla A pair of small drums.

Notes for teachers

pp4–5 The Sikh religion was founded by Guru Nanak, who was born in India in 1469. At that time, the main religions in India were Islam and Hinduism. Guru Nanak disagreed with elements of his Hindu religion, such as the caste system. He announced that 'There is neither Hindu nor Muslim, only God's path.' Guru Nanak believed there was a new way to serve God by praying, working hard and helping people. He taught that all people were equal, regardless of colour, class or gender. Guru Nanak was followed by nine more human Gurus.

pp6–7 Although no particular day of the week is holier than the others, Sangraand, the first day of each Indian lunar calendar month, is important. Many Sikhs visit the gurdwara for special prayers, usually early in the morning. Sikhs generally visit the gurdwara on the holy day in the country they live in; for example, they go on Fridays in Muslim countries. After worship, everyone sits and eats langar together, as a reminder that all people are equal. Volunteers cook and serve the food, which is always vegetarian so everyone can eat it.

pp8–9 Sikh melas coincide with Hindu festivals. Gurpurbs are special to the Sikhs. Vaisakhi is the most important mela because it celebrates the birth of the Khalsa, the Sikh community. There were ten human Gurus, so there are a large number of gurpurbs. All gurpurbs give Sikhs the opportunity to rededicate themselves to their religion. They give money to charity and may offer free food and services (such as medical or dental check-ups) to the community.

pp10–11 The Khalsa was founded in 1699. At Vaisakhi, which was the celebration of the Indian New Year, Guru Gobind Singh, the tenth Guru, asked for the heads of five Sikhs. Five brave Sikhs stepped forward, but the Guru did not kill them; this was a test of their faith. They became the first five members of the Khalsa. The Amrit ceremony marks a Sikh's entry into the religious community and does not take place until they are at least 14. When they join the community, they promise to worship one God and follow the Gurus' teachings.

pp12–13 The Sikh flag-pole is washed in yoghurt to symbolize purity. The Khanda is significant: the double-edged sword in the centre represents God; the circle

symbolizes eternity, or the continuity of life; the two swords represent spiritual and political power in the world. In large UK cities, such as Birmingham, there are huge processions and celebrations, including bhangra dancing. Each procession is led by five Sikhs to commemorate the first members of the Khalsa. Bhangra originated with Vaisakhi in the Punjab, which was also a harvest festival. The dance tells the story of farmers' lives.

pp14–15 At the start of the seventeenth century, Emperor Jehangir of India accused Guru Arjan of including attacks on Muslims and Hindus in the Sikh holy book he had compiled, the Adi Granth. Guru Arjan denied this. He was tortured and killed. The cool drinks, given to all at this gurpurb, irrespective of religion, remind people how Guru Arjan stayed calm and cool despite being tortured in boiling water. Many Sikhs have been martyred for their religion.

pp16–17 The Guru Granth Sahib, always 1,430 pages long, is a compilation of hymns called shabads, written by the Sikh Gurus, and also includes many hymns written by Hindu and Muslim holy men. The hymns, which are in Gurmukhi, a written form of the Punjabi language, are poems that can be sung to music. The Guru Granth Sahib is treated with the reverence that Sikhs showed to the human Gurus in their time.

pp18–19 Divali is also a Hindu festival, but it has a different meaning for Sikhs. In the seventeenth century, Har Gobind was imprisoned because Emperor Jehangir believed he was plotting against him. When his release was ordered, he refused to leave prison unless 52 Hindu princes jailed alongside him were also released; he succeeded in freeing them. Guru Har Gobind then travelled to Amritsar, arriving at Divali time. He was welcomed by Sikhs holding candles and lamps. Since then, the Divali lights have symbolized freedom for Sikhs.

pp20–21 The reading of the Guru Granth Sahib all the way through is called Akhand Path, and it is undertaken on all festivals and special occasions. It means 'unbroken reading'. Sikhs try to attend part of the reading, perhaps going to the gurdwara on their way home from work or school. Sikh communities hold a procession through the streets, led by five people who represent the first five members of the Khalsa. The Guru Granth Sahib is carried through the streets on a covered litter.

pp22–3 In the late seventeenth century, Emperor Aurangzeb wanted all the people of India to convert to Islam. Guru Tegh Bahadur said that if the emperor could convert him, then all the Hindus would convert, too. Even under torture, the Guru refused, and he was beheaded. Guru Tegh Bahadur's message was that it is right to sacrifice yourself for other people. This festival is celebrated mainly in New Delhi and in gurdwaras dedicated to Guru Tegh Bahadur. The gurdwara built where the Guru was martyred in 1675 is called Gurdwara Sisganj, and is the focal point for the celebrations.

pp24–5 Guru Gobind Singh is the second most important Guru after Guru Nanak. His family suffered because they would not convert to Islam; the Guru's four sons and his father were killed. Guru Gobind Singh was an excellent poet and an accomplished musician. Music forms an essential part of Sikh worship – traditional instruments are the tabla (a pair of drums) and the harmonium. The Five Ks are the Sikh 'uniform' introduced by Guru Gobind Singh.

pp26–7 At the Hindu festival of Holi, Hindus enjoy boisterous celebrations. The tenth Guru, Guru Gobind Singh, introduced a Sikh version of the festival in 1680; he thought it was a good opportunity to perform mock battles to train Sikhs to defend themselves. Traditionally, Sikhs are supposed to do sport to keep fit. The main place where Hola Mohalla is celebrated today is Anandpur, in the Punjab, India. There is a big carnival and a procession with people carrying the Nishan Sahib. Similar celebrations are held outside the Punjab and in the West.

p28 The timing of Sikh festivals is fixed according to the lunar calendar. Vaisakhi is the only Sikh festival that is fixed according to the solar year.

Other resources

Artefacts

Articles of Faith, Resource House, Kay Street, Bury BL9 6BU Tel. 0161 763 6232
Degh Tegh Fateh, 117 Soho Road, Handsworth, Birmingham B21 9ST Tel. 0121 515 1183
Supplies pictures and Sikh music.

Religion in Evidence, 28b Nunnbrook Road Industrial Estate, Huthwaite, Nottinghamshire NG17 2HU
Tel. 0800 318686
The Sikh Missionary Society, 10 Featherstone Road, Southall, Middlesex UB2 5AA Tel. 020 8574 1902
Supplies free literature and stocks artefacts.

Books to read

Celebrations: Baisakhi by Mandy Ross (Heinemann, 2001)
Celebration Stories: The Guru's Family – A Story about Guru Nanak's Birthday by Pratima Mitchell (Hodder Wayland, 2002)
Great Religious Leaders: Guru Nanak and Sikhism by Rajinder Singh Panesar (Hodder Wayland, 2002)
Keystones: Sikh Gurdwara by Kanwaljit Kaur-Singh (A&C Black, 2000)
My Belief: I am a Sikh by M. Aggarwal (Franklin Watts, 2001)
My Life, My Religion: Sikh Granthi by Kanwaljit Kaur-Singh (Franklin Watts, 2001)
Places of Worship: Sikh Gurdwaras by Gopinder Kaur (Heinemann, 2000)
Storyteller: Sikh Stories by Anita Ganeri (Evans, 2001)
What Do We Know About Sikhism? by Beryl Dhanjal (Hodder Wayland, 1996)
Where We Worship: Sikh Gurdwara by Kanwaljit Kaur-Singh (Franklin Watts, 1998)

Posterpack

Living Religions: Sikhism Posterpack and booklet by Thomas Nelson and Sons.

Videos

Animated World Faiths for ages 7–12 (Channel 4)
Pathways of Belief for ages 7–11 (BBC)
Stop, Look and Listen: 'Water, Moon, Candle, Tree and Sword' for KS1 (Channel 4)

Websites

For websites that are relevant to this book, go to:
www.waylinks.co.uk/yearfestivalssikh

Index